How to Manage in Times of Crisis

ADDITIONAL WORKS BY THE AUTHOR

Managing Corporate Lifecycles: An Updated and Expanded Look at the classic work *Corporate Lifecycles* (2004)

The Ideal Executive: Why You Cannot Be One and What To Do About It: A New Paradigm for Management (2004)

Management/Mismanagement Styles: How to Identify a Style and What to Do About It (2004)

Leading the Leaders: How to Enrich Your Style of Management and Handle People Whose Style is Different from Yours (2004)

The Pursuit of Prime (1996)

Mastering Change: The Power of Mutual Trust and Respect in Personal Life, Family, Business and Society (1993)

How to Solve the Mismanagement Crisis (1979)

Self-Management: New Dimensions to Democracy (with Elisabeth Mann-Borgese) (1975)

Industrial Democracy, Yugoslav Style: The Effect of Decentralization on Organizational Behavior (1971)

To view a full list of all available Adizes Institute publications, or to place an order, please visit
www.adizes.com/store

How to Manage in Times of Crisis

(And How to Avoid a Crisis in the First Place)

ICHAK KALDERON ADIZES, PH.D.
Founder, Adizes Institute
Santa Barbara, California

© 2009 Dr. Ichak Adizes

Published by
Adizes Institute Publications
1212 Mark Avenue
Carpinteria
Santa Barbara County, California, USA 93013
805-565-2901; Fax 805-565-0741
Website: www.adizes.com

All rights reserved. No part of this publication may
be reproduced in any form, by any means (including
electronic, photocopying, recording or otherwise), without
permission of the author and the publisher.

Library of Congress Control Number: 2009902144

ISBN: 978-0-937120-09-5

Design and layout by RJ Communications LLC, New York
Printed in the United States of America

Additional copies may be ordered from www.adizes.com.

Acknowledgments

I want to thank my associates Nebojsa Caric (Adizes South East Europe), Sunil Dovedy (Adizes USA), and Carlos Valdesuso (Adizes Brazil) for their most helpful comments on an early draft. My thanks go to Nan Goldberg for editing my speech and Emily Garvin for copy editing the final draft.

Recognition

The following is an edited version of a presentation made at IBS—the Academy of Economics of the Russian Federation—on November 14, 2008. Dr. Adizes is the honorary scientific advisor to IBS, from which he received an honorary doctorate in 2007.

A crisis can be a real blessing to any person, to any nation, for all crises bring progress.

Creativity is born from anguish, just as the day is born from the dark night.

It is in crisis that inventiveness, discoveries, and grand strategies are born.

He who overcomes crisis overcomes himself, without himself being overcome.

He who blames his failure on a crisis neglects his own talent, and is more respectful of problems than of solutions.

The true crisis is the crisis of incompetence.

The greatest fault of both people and nations is the laziness with which they attempt to find the solutions to their problems.

There is no challenge without crisis.

And without challenges, life becomes a routine, a slow death.

Without crisis, there is no merit. It's in a crisis that we can show the very best in us, because without crises every wind becomes a mere caress.

To speak about a crisis is to promote it, and yet to be silent about a crisis is to promote conformity.

Let us work hard instead. Let us stop, once and for all, the crisis of our tragic unwillingness to overcome challenges.

– Albert Einstein

RIGHT NOW, IN 2009, the world is in a deep financial crisis. It affects everyone, particularly companies that are undergoing a transformation into an increasingly competitive economy and experiencing rapid and continual economic, political, and technological changes: companies that must have access to credit in order to continue developing.

In general, people don't like crises. Although the dictionary meaning of "crisis" is an upheaval or turning point that causes a decisive change—for worse or for better—the word usually has a negative connotation. When people hear the word "crisis," they automatically assume it's a disaster. Most people dread crises, and that goes even more for managers of organizations, who must worry about protecting their organizations' existence.

But it doesn't have to be that way. And here is why.

Let us start with an analogy. You probably remember that back when you were a child, your parents told you, "Do not take a hot shower and then go outside in the cold weather! You will catch a cold!" Well, I always wondered why *I* would catch a cold if I went outside with wet hair in freezing temperatures, while in Finland and Russia people like to go to the sauna, sweat, then go outside and roll in the snow. It makes them feel invigorated! Some people in Siberia, including the aged, dig a hole in the ice on a lake or river, then dive into the freezing water—and they also feel invigorated! If I did that I would probably get pneumonia and die.

Why the difference?

What we have to realize is that it's not the cold that makes us sick. It is the rapid *change* from hot to cold. But that still doesn't explain why people in Finland become invigorated by the quick change from hot to cold, while the same change makes me sick.

It's all about the strength, or lack of strength, of your organism. If your organism is robust, change makes you stronger. But if you're weak, change can kill you.

This phenomenon does not apply only to people but to organizations, too. Organizations that are prepared to deal with change are invigorated by it. Those that are not fall ill and risk bankruptcy.

What does it mean to have a "strong organism"? Does it mean to have big muscles? No. It means that the organism is strong enough to deal with change. It is strength not of physique but of the capacity to handle change.

In order to understand what it means to have a strong organization that is capable of handling change, we should first discuss how change causes organizational "diseases." By understanding the causes of problems created by change, we will be able to identify the appropriate remedy.

Change is nothing new. Change has been here forever, for billions of years. What is new is that the rate of change is accelerating, faster and faster and faster… Our grandparents probably made one strategic decision in their lifetimes (to move to a new city, change jobs, etc.), and our parents made strategic decisions every fifteen or twenty years. We might make strategic decisions every ten years, and most probably, our children are going to make strategic decisions every couple of years, maybe even every year.

The nature of change and its repercussions

THE INCREASING RATE of change has repercussions. When change occurs, problems arise: what to do in the new situation or with the new events facing us. As change accelerates, problems are attacking us faster. Everybody has more problems than they can handle. People are falling behind faster and getting more and more stressed.

But when we solve the problem, what happens? The solution itself is a cause of change, which now creates new problems. So, the more problems we solve—guess what? —the more problems we have. The end result is that we will always have problems.

Why can't we have *no* problems? People often have expectations that if only they follow *this* system, if only they follow *this* religion, if only they follow *this* book, if only they follow *this* ideology—if only they do this or that— they will have no more problems. That is the promise of all religions and all political ideologies.

But that's utopian. The truth is, you can stop having problems only when there is no more change. And that means when you are…dead. Dead! Think about it: The quietest place in town is the cemetery. Nothing is happening there. To be alive, by definition, means to have problems. If you don't have problems, don't worry, they're on their way. Life *is* problems. Why? Because change creates problems, and change is life. (A Google search produced 3.8 million hits for the expression "Life's a bitch and then you die.") Only when there is no life will there be no change, and only then will we have no problems. Or at least that is what we *think*—because so far no one has come back from the hereafter and told us differently.

Problems come with the territory called living, and the faster the rate of change in your life or your company, the more problems you will have.

> *So, your first Take-home Value is:*
>
> *If you have problems, relax! You are in good company. You are alive. And if you believe you don't have problems, then your biggest problem could be that you do not recognize your problems.*

I once had a client in the software business. The company grew very rapidly: 100 percent a year. When its managers complained to me about how many problems they had, I asked them, "What do you expect? With that rate of growth and, thus, change, you *must* have lots of problems. That is normal."

It is normal to have problems. We have already covered that. But when you cannot handle a problem caused by change—aha!—now you have a problem that is abnormal. And if you do not solve the abnormal problems, over time they can become fatal problems. That is what is happening to the big automotive companies of Detroit. They have been so slow in responding to market needs, for so long, that now no loans or donations will save them. Why? Because they are no longer facing normal problems. Now they seem to be facing fatal problems.

Problems change in their severity over time. But having bigger problems does not necessarily mean that the situation is worse.

One year I sent a greeting card to all my clients wishing them a happy and productive new year. My wish was:

> *"May you have **bigger** problems in the coming year than the ones you had this passing year…"*

At the bottom of the card in small letters, it read:

> *"… that you can handle successfully."*

You are as big as the problems you can handle. So having bigger problems is not a sign of dying, it is a sign of growing. Let us assume that this year you face the problem of how to successfully sell your product regionally. Several years later, you have the bigger problem of how to manage sales nationally; still later, you have problems managing an international company; and eventually you face the problem of how to convert an international company into a well-managed multinational.

The problems are getting bigger, but it is because you are taking on bigger assignments. You are growing.

When you have smaller and smaller problems, it means your strength is declining. You are aging.

Of course, when you have bigger and bigger problems that you cannot handle, it means you are dying.

When there is change, are you capable of dealing with it? How change will affect you depends on you. If you can handle problems successfully, they aren't problems anymore. They are opportunities, because, in reality, every problem is also an opportunity.

In the Chinese language, the word for "problem" and the word for "opportunity" are one and the same! There is no difference. And doesn't that make sense? What is your opportunity? Your client or competitor's problem. For them it's a problem, but for you it is an opportunity. And what is your competitor's opportunity? *Your* problem, which he knows how to address better than you do.

But why would you want to make your problem somebody else's opportunity? Why don't you make your problem your *own* opportunity?

Please note: Whether change becomes a problem or an opportunity depends on what you do with it. It is as if this new situation demands of you: "Do you want me to be a problem or an opportunity? You decide. If you don't do what you need to do, I will be a problem. If you react appropriately, I will be an opportunity. Which do you want me to be?"

Definition of a "crisis"

SO FAR WE have talked about "problems" caused by change. What about "crises"?

Henry Kissinger once said that a problem that goes untreated is a crisis in waiting. It makes sense, does it not? For example, this worldwide financial crisis we are in now was not born last week or last month. It began with problems that were left untreated over time. Problems are like shadows: If you turn around and chase them, they run away from you. But if *you* run away from *them*, they chase you, and sooner or later they catch up. In other words, if we ignore our problems or don't solve them quickly enough, they will grow bigger and bigger and eventually turn into crises.

A crisis has the same characteristics as problems caused by change, except it is more acute—a more intense change with more profound implications for the organization. The weak will die faster. To succeed, we'll need to act better and faster.

The longer we wait to deal with a problem, the higher the probability that it will turn into a crisis, in which case we will have to be reactive. That is like driving forward while looking through the rear window.

Notice that the environmental change that's causing

the crisis involves *your competition*, too, not just you; thus, everybody has the same problem or is given the same opportunity. Who is going to survive? Those who are more capable of adapting to change. Crises will make the weak die faster and the strong grow stronger. So the key to making a crisis into an opportunity is to be strong *before* the crisis develops. Then, as the weak die off, your strength will sustain you and may even increase.

Please note: Since problems are opportunities, and a crisis is a more acute problem, then it follows that a crisis is also a more accentuated opportunity.

Now, what does it mean to deal with change and crisis better than the competition? How can a company exploit opportunities when it feels it is up to its chin in trouble because of the crisis?

Don't despair. Help is on its way. Keep reading.

The importance of timely reaction

TWO MEN WENT on a walking safari in Africa. As they were walking, they saw a lion approaching. One of them immediately started putting on his running shoes. His companion, surprised, asked, "Why are you putting your running shoes on? You can't outrun a lion!" The first one said, "I am not trying to outrun the lion; I am trying to outrun you!"

How fast are *you* on your feet? How fast can *you* change?

Years ago, I was consulting for Porsche. Peter Schultz, the then-president, who became a very good friend of mine, told me an interesting story:

As soon as he was appointed president of Porsche SE, he went to visit all the different departments to introduce himself. At the engineering department, he asked in passing, "Do we [Porsche] compete in Le Mans?" (Le Mans is a world-famous annual car-racing event.) "Oh, no!" the engineering staff replied. "We don't compete in Le Mans; that is beyond us."

Schultz decided there and then to show his leadership. He said, "We are a sports car company, so we *will* compete in Le Mans next year. I am giving you, the engineering department, the challenge to compete, and I rely on you to win the race next year."

The engineers took their orders seriously. They worked night and day to develop the engine, design the car, and test it. They went to Le Mans, competed, and won.

Big celebration! They were very happy, but it was short-lived. The Le Mans racing committee unexpectedly changed the rules for the next year's race, which meant that Porsche's engineers would have to start from scratch to design and test a new car.

The engineers were demoralized. But Schultz was elated. "We should be glad they changed the rules!" he said. "They didn't change them only for us; they changed them for everyone. Who will win this time? Who will succeed? The answer is: those who are faster and better at dealing with change. And the weak ones will fail."

His next, very simple sentence has become one of my managerial mantras: "If there is no change, the mediocre catch up!"

Let me repeat: If there is no change, the mediocre catch up. They learn from the winners, and eventually they win competitions that you used to win. But if you are strong, change gives you the opportunity to move forward and leave the competition behind. If you are strong, a crisis may be your ally!

> *Take-home Value No. 2:*
>
> *Crisis is good for excellent leaders and companies—those who can successfully deal with change—because in a crisis, their weaker competitors die and leave the market to them.*

One element of being "strong" is that you can make prompt changes in your organization. You are not an aircraft carrier that needs five miles to turn around; you are a PT boat, which can turn in no time.

But as far as organizations are concerned, the speed with which you can change direction is not a function of size. In this book, I will illustrate how to be an aircraft carrier that can turn around like a PT boat.

In other words, we need to be more agile, to change faster than our competition—or at least as fast as the market is changing.

How?

Many books on management talk about adapting to a changing environment. Adapting, to me, means to be reactive: You wait until you know what is happening and then you adapt. It works if the change is slow. But if the change is rapid, adapting could be too late: By the time you adapt, the environment has changed again. You are always behind and thus out of touch with your market.

Have you ever tried playing tennis reactively, going to the ball only after it lands? You will not hit too many balls, right? You need to predict where the ball is going to land and proactively position yourself on the court. It's the same for companies. The way to "stay in the game" and win is to be better at pro-acting to change.

If an untreated problem is a crisis in waiting, then it follows that if we are successful in treating emerging problems proactively, they will not become crises.

> *Take-home Value No. 3:*
>
> *If we treat our problems proactively and effectively, we will survive better than if we react to those problems.*

Now, assume that a company is willing to act—either to pro-act or, if it is too late to pro-act, to react to the crisis. What, exactly, should it *do*?

To answer this question, let us address why change

gives birth to problems or opportunities. Understanding the cause will help us find the remedy.

Why change causes problems

EVERYTHING IS A SYSTEM. Everything. Even you, as a person, are a system. The sky is a system, too. If you are an astrophysicist, you understand the system that determines how the stars move or relate to one another.

Whenever you have a system, by definition you have a set of sub-systems that comprise the system. And every sub-system has its own sub-systems, and so on, ad infinitum.

When there is change, the sub-systems do not change in synchronicity. Some change faster than others. That creates gaps. Those gaps are manifested by what we call "problems." If we don't treat those gaps quickly enough, the problems become a crisis.

Let me illustrate with an example. Let's take you as a person, and then extrapolate to companies, and then to society. As a person, you are a system composed of many, many sub-systems. One way to identify the sub-systems is as the physical you, the intellectual you, the emotional you, and the spiritual you.

All these separate aspects of you don't necessarily change together. Let's say you're 47 years old, and your body—your physical sub-system—functions approximately like a normal 47-year-old person.

But while you're 47 physically, you might be

intellectually about 70. How? Your education and experience in the world are more sophisticated than the average 47-year-old. You're wiser than your age. People often say of you, "He has a very wise old soul."

And while you're 47 physically and 70 years old intellectually, emotionally you may still be a teenager: "When are you going to grow up? Enough with all this adolescent behavior!" your spouse may complain.

Meanwhile, at the same time that you are 17 years old emotionally, 47 physically, and 70 years intellectually, it's possible that spiritually, you haven't even been born yet.

That creates problems. Why? Because you are not *together*. Your sub-systems are misaligned. You as a person are *disintegrating*. You are falling apart. Despite your intelligence and wisdom, you still behave like a child. People conclude, "He is not mature enough!"

The same is true for a company. For example, in a young company, marketing and sales change direction very fast, responding to changes in the marketplace. Why? Because they need clients. They will do anything for a client. If their client wants to go left, they go left; if the client prefers to go right, then right is where they go. They need the money, so they follow the market.

While marketing and sales are very flexible and changing rapidly, accounting usually remains in the Stone Age. They change *veeery slooowly*. And the human resource function may barely exist. That creates problems for a company, and if the company does not deal with this increasing disintegration, the time of reckoning will come.

With disintegration spreading, the faster the company grows into new markets with new products, the less information top management has; thus increasingly it works in the dark. With incomplete or even wrong information, management could, and often does, make bad decisions, with disastrous financial results. Sales could be going up while profit is going down, and management won't even know why. And because HR considerations have not been taken into account, the company keeps hiring tomorrow the people it needed yesterday. Staff is unprepared, tasks are not delegated, and the various departments don't communicate. This company's sub-systems are advancing at different speeds, and because management is busy focusing exclusively on the market and ignoring the other sub-systems, the company is developing a lot of problems it probably won't deal with until those problems become crises. And that is only a question of time.

This is equally true for a country. In the United States, for example, the economic/financial sub-system is changing, and the technological sub-system is changing even faster. Today, in the 21st century, there are already more living scientists than throughout the rest of history combined. More innovations were made in the 20th century than cumulatively in the history of civilization. We are changing very, very fast.

Yet, while technologies are changing very fast, and the economy is changing fast, our values change slowly. That creates social and political problems. We live in a technological society, a term the philosopher Jacques Ellul coined as early as 1949, but our value systems still correspond to some distant past. We have atomic bombs but we fight wars according to values similar to those of primitive man.

Change causes disintegration. And the more extreme the change, the faster things fall apart. Show me a house on the beach, where the climate frequently changes from one extreme to the other, and I will show you a house that is falling apart faster than normal. You need to pro-act even more. You need to do more preventive maintenance than usual, and if you do none, you will have a crisis: the house will become uninhabitable.

Disintegration is universal and inevitable

WE ARE NOT talking only about business here. *All* problems are caused by disintegration. When you have a problem—*any* problem—something is falling apart. If you have a physical problem, you need to go to a doctor: Something in your body is falling apart. If you have psychological problems, something in your emotional life is disintegrating. If you have family problems, something is falling apart in your family. If your car is not running as it should, you need to take it to a mechanic: Something is disintegrating.

When we're worried about someone or something, what do we say? "This person is falling apart." "This family is falling apart." "This company is falling apart." "This country is falling apart." Or sometimes, "He is coming unglued." These are all expressions describing disintegration.

The faster the changes, the faster the disintegration and the more problems you will have.

I've noticed something very interesting: The higher the rate of change in a country, or even a city or region, the higher the rate of divorce. Families fall apart.

Why do so many families fall apart and end up divorcing in times of crisis? Because in a crisis they have to solve their problems quickly and rationally, and they are not always well equipped to do that.

First, they have to decide what to do. This is when differences in style come to the surface. One thinks this way; the other thinks that way, etc. There are differences in needs and in interests that need to be handled, as well. The result is a lot of stress because those differences have to be dealt with under pressure, which increases the stress, and thus the pain.

Countries fall apart, too, as the forces of change prevail and cause rapid disintegration. Whatever system we are talking about—you as a human being, family, business, or society—the same principles apply.

Take the financial crisis that began in the United States in 2008. What happened? For the previous decade, at least, many people were taking mortgages beyond their means, assuming that the value of their homes would continue to appreciate and justify the risk they were taking. The banks gave those loans under the same assumptions, and then pooled many of these mortgage loans together, packaged ("securitized") them, and sold them on the stock market. The buyers of those packages insured the securitized portfolio of mortgages against default. The insurance companies took a calculated risk for a hefty premium, and probably re-insured themselves.

All looks well. Right?

What was really happening, however, was a disintegration of how risk was handled. Before, the risk was taken on only by the bank; now, it is spread among the borrower, the bank, the stock market investors, and the insurance companies. When the risk migrated and split into multiple components, no one could see the whole picture, much less keep it under control. The credit system fell apart.

"Lies, damned lies, and statistics"

I REMEMBER ASKING A banker years ago, "How can you sell these securitized mortgages? How can people know how good the mortgages are?" It seemed clear to me that it was impossible for people who were buying security-backed mortgages to estimate how much risk they were taking, because there was no way to tell how safe the mortgages were until they were paid.

The banker said: "They check it; they do sampling."

Well, as Mark Twain once famously said, "There are three kinds of lies: lies, damned lies, and statistics."

Statistics can be manipulated in nearly infinite ways. Even if checking and sampling is done, you just don't know whether past conditions will continue into the future, or how long the economy will continue growing, and thus when the time of reckoning will come.

When the housing market bubble burst and home prices fell, there was a domino effect: All those mortgage packages were suddenly recognized to be at risk, and no one had the vast resources to cover the risk.

In my opinion, it was not greed that caused the crisis. Greed is actually what fuels the economy: Without greed, people would not work hard building assets and building empires. So one should not vilify greed. Besides, in a competitive economy the leaders who are less "greedy" get fired if they do not take every opportunity to make money for their companies.

> *Take-home Value No. 4:*
>
> *All problems are caused by disintegration, which is caused by change. A crisis is a manifestation of prolonged, untreated disintegration.*

I believe what caused the crisis was a change in the financial markets' structure and instruments. The changes caused disintegration, which was not handled promptly. Why? Because there was no precedent that could alert those in charge to do something about it proactively.

So what could have been a normal problem became an abnormal problem and eventually a crisis.

When you take your car to the mechanic for a diagnosis, what is he going to look for? Whatever it is that's falling apart! And how does he repair the car? He puts it back together. What is a healer supposed to do with the problems you present to him or her? Put you together! Note that the verbs "to heal" and "to make whole" come from the same root. That's why psychologists say "oneness or illness," and, in English at least, when we praise somebody, what do we say? "This person has it all together!" When we admire some family, we say "Wow! This family really has it together!" We even say, "This country has it together."

The remedy

HOW DO WE put things together? If change causes disintegration, and disintegration is the cause of problems, what is the solution?

Integration.

Organizations that are well integrated will weather the storm better than those that are already disintegrating. A united family can weather a crisis better than a family that was dysfunctional from the start.

But how do you achieve integration?

The most effective way, which gets you first prize, is to integrate proactively, not reactively. Another, less successful method—second prize—is to integrate reactively, after the problem has appeared on the radar. The booby prize goes to those who ignore the problem—even though it is blinking on the radar screen and screaming for attention—until it is a crisis, and then, and *only* then, begin dealing with it. And no prize whatsoever goes to those who freeze, do nothing, allowing the crisis to take over the organization and cause its demise.

Whether you act proactively or reactively to achieve integration, you have to do the same thing. The only differences are the speed with which you have to act and the degree of complexity you will be facing. The longer you wait to deal with disintegration, the more you will have to deal with it "under fire" and the more complex the treatment will have to be. The longer you wait, the more sub-systems will become involved and the more complex the problem itself becomes.

> *Take-home Value No. 5, then, is:*
>
> *The treatment for disintegration is integration, and integration is best achieved proactively, by learning how to predict problems and solve them before they become crises.*

The treatment is to look for what is falling apart or not working smoothly, and figure out how to put it together effectively and efficiently. Management must proactively change and synchronize the sub-systems. That is what makes the organization strong.

To be proactive is the best solution, because if you are ready for a problem, it is not a problem. It's a task, a job to do. It is not a surprise. A problem, on the other hand, is a surprise that takes your energy away, hits you in the stomach and shoves the air out of your lungs. You're going along, everything is wonderful, then *BOOM!* You did not expect it. *That's* a problem. And a problem you knew existed but ignored will become a crisis. Now it does not hit you in the stomach. It brings you to your knees.

Be proactive. Do not wait.

Here is an analogy: A woman went to a psychotherapist and asked him when she should start treating her 18-year-old son's problems. The therapist responded, "Eighteen years ago! You don't wait until there is trouble. You start the day he is born!"

Same thing with a company: You don't wait until the problem says, "Hello, here I am!" It is much better to prepare for it in advance, so when it arrives, you can say, "I've been waiting for you. I am ready. Thank you! Next!"

What *not* to do

THE WORST CHOICE, the one for which there is no prize, is to do nothing, to freeze in fear, to accuse the wind and the weather—or worse, to cover up and disguise the problems with actions that make the organization look good, while in reality the source of the problems—i.e., increasing disintegration—remains untreated and eventually will become a crisis. Some organizations do nothing because they are waiting for the situation to clear up. They are waiting for the storm to pass.

Wrong.

When you have a crisis in your personal life, you have a lot of pain, don't you? What do you do when you have a lot of pain? Classically, what happens is you freeze, you hold your breath. And what happens when you stop breathing? You have more pain! Any time you have physical pain, what do the doctors, your mother, and your spouse all tell you? *Breathe! Breathe!!!* And when you do start to breathe, the pain dissipates. It helps to bring oxygen to your body.

So when there is a crisis, *act*. Do not freeze.

Another analogy: You are walking down the street and you come to an intersection. That's change, something new. Now you have to decide whether to turn left or right, go straight ahead, or go back. If you decide not to decide—"I don't know what to do… I don't have the information… I cannot decide!"—you've still made a decision. To do what? To stay where you are. And that might be the worst decision for you.

It is OK to do nothing if you make that decision consciously, as part of your strategy to choose the timing of your actions. It is not OK to just freeze because you do not know what to do.

There is an American expression: "Even if you are on the right road, if you just stand there, you may be run over by a truck!" When there is a crisis, doing nothing is the worst thing you can do. The pain increases, the fear increases, and eventually you might even experience hysteria. You need to *do* something instead. And hesitating because you fear failure is not an option.

> *Take-home value No. 6:*
> *Not making a decision is making a decision—to do nothing. Doing nothing out of fear is a prescription for an eventual crisis.*

Mary Kay was a very famous American entrepreneur who started from nothing and built a very, very big cosmetics empire, Mary Kay Cosmetics, by selling door-to-door. Starting from zero, her company earned millions. So people often asked her, "Miss Mary Kay, what is the secret of your success?" And she replied, "Do you want to see the scars on my knees? That is the secret of my success!" Success is not about how rarely you fall down. Success is about how quickly you get up.

We all fall, sooner or later. And some of us fall frequently. It depends on how daring we are.

Many people believe that success means not falling: "I'll never make a mistake!" *That* is your biggest mistake! When there is a crisis and you find you are falling, don't freeze. Get up! Get up!!! *This* is your time to move—to run faster than your competitors, so that the lion will eat them and not you.

George Soros, one of the richest men on earth, once said, "I am not smarter than anybody else; I just identify my mistakes faster and correct them faster." In contrast, by the time most people recognize a problem and do something about it, either the window of opportunity has passed, or the problem has grown more acute and become a crisis.

> *Take-home value No. 7:*
>
> *Success is not defined by not making mistakes. Success is defined by how quickly you identify and correct your mistakes.*

Many years ago the Australians competed for the America's Cup, the world's most prestigious regatta and match race in the sport of sailing. Alan Bond, who owned the Australian competing boat, invited me to the finals and also asked me to stay in his home. It was to honor me, he told me, because he had used my methodology of complementary team building to build his team. (They won!)

During dinner he received a phone call. When he came back he looked a bit upset.

"Alan, what happened?" I asked him.

"Oh, I just got the news that I lost twenty million dollars on a deal."

"How does it feel to lose twenty million dollars?" I asked sincerely, because it was more than my total net worth.

"You know, Ichak," he said, "I look at it this way: I have just taken a course in the University of Life whose tuition was twenty million dollars. First, there are not many people who can afford a course that costs twenty million dollars. So I am one of a very few. From that point of view, I am happy I can afford such tuition. Second, now that I paid the tuition, the question is did I pass the course, did I learn anything from it? Or did I fail the course?"

A crisis, a problem, should be seen as a course in the university called life. Each problem is a course and there is always tuition. Now the question is: Did you waste the tuition and learn nothing, or did you get the full value of the course?

OK, learning is important. What else is important?

> *Take-home Value No. 8:*
>
> *What are you learning from the problem or crisis you're dealing with? Regard each crisis as an opportunity to learn valuable lessons.*

You must be proactive. You have to be urgent. You have to keep moving.

But moving to do what?

To keep the company together—integrated—in times of change. To fight the disintegration that change brings.

So what should you, as a parent or as an executive, do during a time of crisis, when you have to truly lead? Can you keep your company together? Can you stop people from attacking one another?

In a strong company, people join together. In America, that's called "circling the wagons": We turn our backs to one another and fight the enemy. But for that you need to trust that the fellow members of your organization will not shoot you in the back.

In a badly managed company, or society, what I described earlier as a "weak organism," people do not trust one another. As the enemy is attacking, it is easier to attack each other than the enemy. A witch-hunt is in full force. But when we attack each other, what happens? The enemy has a better opportunity to kill us all. So in times of crisis, more than any other time, trust is at a premium.

Integration has many dimensions.

Many years ago I had a client who lost all his assets in the 1990s real estate crisis in the United States. He was a wealthy man who ended up having to borrow money from his daughter to buy food.

He nevertheless looked fine to me. Not what you would expect from a person who had lost everything. He was upbeat.

"Moises," I asked him, "how do you keep your spirits up when you've lost everything?"

"I did not lose everything," he said. "Only money. I did not lose my real assets: my health, my family, and my friends. As long as I have that, I will recoup the money."

And he did. Years later I met him, and he was again the rich man that he used to be.

In a crisis, people lose more than money. They lose their health. Their families could fall apart, and they might even lose their friends.

So, in a crisis, your first priority is your health. The pain you feel from the stress can make you vulnerable to serious illnesses. Keep yourself together, first and above all. Think of the instructions you get on an airplane about what to do in an emergency. Even if you are with a child, what do they say? Put the oxygen mask on your face first; then take care of others. If you are falling apart, how can you take care of others? So take care of yourself first.

How do you keep yourself together in times of crisis? One way I recommend is to meditate. Slow down. Don't panic. Just meditate for a few minutes a day. (Make sure you know the correct way to do it.)

Next, keep your family together. Give hope. Show leadership in your personal life. Don't run around scared, spreading your hysteria to those who depend on you.

Third, call your friends. See if they are in a worse situation than you are. Help them if you can, and ask for their help if they can offer it.

Once you've got yourself, your family, and your friends together, focus on keeping your company together. Address the fears your employees have. Be honest. Remember, in times of crisis, trust is at a premium. Now is the time when trust will be tested. Do not fail the test. Be honest, truthful, and accountable. Do not camouflage the situation. Do not deny the truth. Do not escape into the world of false promises. People know when you are avoiding the truth. They know in their gut if you are coming clean or not.

Keeping your company together is not enough. Call your clients. Ask them if you can help them. Again, be truthful. No games. No false promises. If you can help them, do. Again, this is when trust is tested. This is when you can reinforce the trust your customers have in you. It is in times of crisis that trust is solidified for life.

Remember, if your clients go bankrupt because of the crisis, you are going to go bankrupt with them. What can you do without clients?

"What does not kill you makes you stronger"

INTEGRATE IN EVERY dimension of your personal and professional life: within yourself, your family, your company, and your clients.

The more you integrate, the stronger you will emerge from the crisis. In retrospect, the crisis could turn out to be the best thing that could have happened to you. It strengthened your family; it made you stronger, more resolute, better disciplined; it built and reinforced your relationships with your clients and customers; it reinforced your relationships with your employees and colleagues.

Act. A crisis is your time to show your true colors as a leader.

The wrong reaction to a crisis is to automatically attribute the cause of the problem to factors outside your control. That is the easy way out. It is one way to avoid dealing with the problem, because what can you do? You cannot treat a problem that is not under your control. But that's like hitting a tree while driving your car and explaining to the insurance company, "I was just driving when all at once this tree jumped in front of me."

> *Take-home value No. 9:*
>
> *In a crisis, instead of attacking each other or blaming outside forces that you cannot control, look inside yourself or your company and focus on how to prevent the organization from falling apart.*

The wiser, not to mention more plausible, approach is not to look outside yourself for the cause of the problem, but to turn around and look inside. *Because that's where the solution is.* It takes much more sophistication and courage to face yourself and ask yourself what is wrong with *you*, instead of what is wrong with the world. You cannot control the outside, but you *can* control the inside. It *is* possible to work inside the company and succeed in controlling it.

Steps to take in a crisis

WHO SURVIVES A crisis? Those who can keep it together. So when a crisis occurs, you have to increase your efforts to keep it together.

But there is a catch. It takes time to integrate a company. Later on we will describe what it really means to "integrate a company," but I assume you already realize intuitively that synchronizing and aligning all the sub-systems, whatever they are, is not a short-term assignment. The danger is that while you as a manager are working on the long-term solution, the company will be going bankrupt in the meantime.

So what do you have to do? You must simultaneously "fight" on multiple fronts. On one hand, you should deal with the urgent manifestations of the crisis, which is usually a cash shortage; and on the other hand, deal with the long-term solution, which is the systemic integration.

Easier said than done, right?

In the current financial crisis, according to a survey by Ernst and Young, companies are reacting as one would expect: firing people (downsizing), and cutting advertising, research and development, training, and consulting. This is both a right and wrong solution. It depends. If this is *only* what companies do, it is a mistake. But if they do that and, at the same time, deal with the integration, it is the right solution.

If they fire good people just to make the numbers look

good, it is as bad as feeding a dog starting with his own tail, until the whole dog disappears.

Let me be more precise. First, we must look reality in the eye: In times of crisis, cash is king. Period. So conserving cash and cutting costs is good. Some companies base their decisions on the information their accrual system gives them. But on an accrual system, you might look good even though your cash flow is not good. My suggestion, in personal life as well as in a company, is to forget relying on accrual accounting. The first step is to do cash-flow projections. I would even say that profit is not as important in the short run as cash, because cash is like blood: If you bleed out, you die.

I always recommend that companies in a crisis do a thirteen-week projection of cash—both inflow and outflow. Thirteen weeks: three months plus one week. At the end of every week, re-forecast using the latest information, adapt your projections for the next twelve weeks, and add another week, so that you're always looking thirteen weeks ahead with information no older than last week.

I was recently in Mexico, where I worked with a very big real estate company. They had been making a typical mistake in times of crisis: They were spending an enormous amount of time trying to secure new loans from the bank. After an analysis, we found out that for them, the cost of capital was very high. Already, the majority of their expenses were financial expenses, the cost of serving the loans they already had. Taking on more debt would be the worst thing to do. They didn't need to spend *more* money on a mortgage, and pay *more* interest. They couldn't afford the interest anyway.

When do you realize you are bankrupt? When you cannot get a loan to pay the interest on your previous loans, that is when your show ends. To avoid that very probable outcome, I suggested to this company that they sell inventory instead. Why? To increase their cash flow. Even if you have to sell at cost, even if you lose money, as long as you cover your variable costs you are contributing to the overhead. It is not a solution for the long run but it buys you time.

Preserve your strengths

THE REAL ESTATE company was about to make another mistake: They were going to fire people.

Be cautious about firing people. Please don't misunderstand me: You definitely should continually comb through your organization and find the people who are not productive, who are not earning their salaries. Find them and get rid of them. But you should have done that a long time ago. Why were you keeping ballast? Why were you keeping people who were not productive? Why does it take a crisis to make you do the cleaning up? Maybe *that* is your problem, that you do not have your finger on the pulse of the organization at all times. Must the company be in crisis for you to pay attention?

But don't fire good people just to cut your costs. That,

by the way, is actually what many traditional consultants recommend doing. They see that you have too many expenses. They put you on a scale and tell you, "You know what? You are 20 pounds overweight; you have to lose 20 pounds." Then they cut off one foot. Now the numbers look very good, but you don't have a foot. I am not talking about a situation in which the company is going bankrupt. In those circumstances, you have gangrene and the foot *must* be cut off. But do not cut a healthy foot in order to show an optimal weight on the scales.

What does a bear do when winter comes? Does it chew off one foot so it will need fewer calories, or does it reduce its metabolism by going into hibernation? What do you personally do in times of financial crisis? Throw one of the kids out on the street so the others can continue eating?

What you *should* do is cut fat, not muscle. If you sacrifice good people, the muscle of your organization, just to make the numbers look good, you are deceiving yourself. How much will it cost you to re-hire and re-train good people later on, when the crisis is over and you need them? Nothing is forever. Conserve your assets so when the upturn occurs, you are ready to roar again.

I once asked Ferdinand Porsche (the son of the car company's founder), "Ferdinand, if you had two choices—to lose all your people or to lose all your machinery—what would you give up first?" What do you think his answer was? "The machinery!"

Why? Which is easier to replace, machines or people? Machines! You buy them, it takes some time to program them, and then they are running. Try to hire people, re-train them, develop the relationships, recreate the culture… How long does *that* take?

Please note: The most difficult thing to do in a company is to build a culture of mutual trust and respect. The easiest thing to lose is a culture of mutual trust and respect, which is indispensable if we are going to turn our backs to one another and fight the enemy. It takes time to build and reinforce such a culture. Sometimes it takes years to find good people, those who know how to disagree without being disagreeable. And how easy is it to do the hiring? Out of ten applicants, maybe you can get three good people—but first you have to find them, then you have to train them, you have to develop them, and then nurture a climate of constructive relationships. And then you fire them? That's like cutting off your foot after investing years in building up its muscles.

Some managers have told me, "I understand that, but it will cost me too much *not* to fire."

It might be true that you cannot afford the cost of labor during the crisis. But is firing the only alternative?

Let's say your business is labor-intensive rather than capital-intensive. Labor really is a major part of your costs. But if your people are talented and productive, and your company is merely suffering a decline in demand, I would recommend that instead of firing people you have everybody work fewer hours. Like the bear in winter, your company should hibernate. The whole organization should share the pain of working and earning less. That includes the top executives. With task sharing, everyone suffers, but only a little bit, and you keep your human assets. After all, that's what you do with your machines when you do not have enough work: You don't go and throw your machines out on the street because you don't have enough work. You leave the machines idle part of the time.

Don't follow the American value system; follow the Japanese system. When companies are in trouble in Japan, the first one to cut his salary is the president. When the company gets into deep trouble, he is the first to resign. In Japan, they don't react by firing the workers, because they believe there are no bad soldiers, only bad generals. Unfortunately, the American system is to fire the workers and let the bad manager stay and even get a bonus.

What should you do with people after you cut their working hours to save cash, but still find that you don't have enough for them to do?

Now is the time to do innovative thinking. Before, when demand was high, your company probably had no time to think creatively about improving your products or services, or adding on to them. It had no time to fix things that were falling apart. Now that there is a slowdown and people have time on their hands, you can give them assignments that will bring innovation to the company. Out of the crisis will emerge a more integrated, more committed, more innovative company than ever before.

In the short or immediate term, conserve cash. Project your cash flow thirteen weeks ahead. Cut your costs—and if that means people, then fire the non-productive and keep the good ones. If you need to cut costs further, turn to task sharing, part-time working. Hibernate and preserve your human assets. Conserve and nurture the culture of mutual trust and respect. Don't violate your values, which were difficult to develop and time-consuming to reinforce.

> *Take-home Value No. 10:*
>
> *In times of crisis, the two most important considerations are to focus on cash flow, and to preserve your organizational culture of mutual trust and respect and the human resources you appreciate.*

If you do fire people, be sure that it is not done in a way that destroys the culture you are trying to preserve.

Those are short-term measures. Now, what about the long run—integration? Disintegration is the source of all evil, remember?

Synchronizing the four sub-systems

IT IS ALWAYS crucial to make sure that integration does not fail in your organization. When there is change, if integration is weak you will fall apart—just like being in a sauna and then going out to roll in the snow and getting pneumonia.

But what do I mean by integration? Should you call up the staff and say, "I love you!"?

Every company, every organization needs to align four sub-systems. Those of you who know my books will recognize the four sub-systems as (P), (A), (E), and (I), but here I will refer to the sub-systems without codifying them, in case readers are not familiar with my books.

The sub-systems that must be integrated at all times are:

1. The teleological sub-system (*telos*, in Greek, means purpose): It is your hierarchy of purposes and what creates those purposes—vision, values, mission, and strategy.
2. The structure of responsibilities: Who is responsible for what, so that the mission of the organization can be achieved.
3. The structure of authority, power, and influence (which I call authorance) in making decisions that lead to change.
4. The reinforcement system, which reinforces behavior so that behavior will be predictable.

All four sub-systems have to be synchronized, more or less, with the changing environment and with each other, over time.

Please note that I said they should not be synchronized exactly, just "more or less." When they are *perfectly* synchronized over time, you are in deep trouble. I'll tell you why very soon.

Reaffirm your mission

SO, FIRST, WHAT are your values? Write a constitution that states what you are going to do, what you are not going to do, what you believe in. What is your mission in light of your vision and values? Make sure to tell everybody you want to hire: "This is our value system, this is what the company stands for, this is what we are trying to do. If you don't share these values, don't work for us."

Restructure responsibilities

WHAT COMES AFTER vision and values? Your mission must be integrated with your structure of responsibilities. "Structure of responsibilities" is usually what we mean when we talk about structure. That is the typical hierarchy of an organization, which states who is responsible for what and to whom.

The right structure of responsibilities is indispensable. In order to deliver the mission and the strategy, the structure of responsibilities must be organized appropriately: If you need to fly, you'd better have an airplane. Too many people make the mistake of trying to make a submarine fly by hiring a pilot to look through the periscope. Yes, you have a pilot, but this is a submarine; it cannot fly.

In other words, the organization should be structured for the mission. Are you a jet plane? Are you a transportation plane? A submarine? What are you? *The form has to follow the function.*

That sounds so simple and obvious, does it not? It isn't. Quite often the company needs to change, so they hire a consultant to do strategic planning. But the consultant is told, "Don't touch the structure." Not even the company president is willing to touch the structure because it is so politically dangerous. "Don't touch the structure; just give me the strategy," they warn the consultant.

But even if you divide responsibilities brilliantly, it is not enough. The structure of responsibilities has an impact, or should have an impact, on how you should allocate authority. Responsibility without authority is a prescription for either becoming apathetic, or developing high blood pressure.

Authorance: Authority, power, and influence

WHEN YOU SAY to somebody, "Show me your organizational structure," they usually show you a chart with boxes and lines. Please realize that this chart represents nothing more than the various divisions of responsibilities. An organization's chart does not tell you who has authority—who the decision-makers really are. It only tells you people's responsibilities and whom they report to.

This brings me to the third subsystem, the structure of authorance (authority, power, and influence). You have to pay attention to the structure of authority and how power and influence undermine it. Who makes, or should make, the decisions, and what about? Maybe the conditions you predict for the future require the company to become more decentralized; or maybe more centralized. Maybe the corporate staff, attempting to protect its interests, is making decisions that impact the operating line, to the disadvantage of the whole organization.

Let us first discuss authority. I define authority as the right to say yes *and* no to decisions that involve change. Usually, people say authority is the right to say "yes" *or* "no." That's wrong. It must be "yes" *and* "no."

Why?

Because if you say "or," it might mean that a person can say "yes" to decisions that involve change, but cannot say "no." But this is rare. What is much more common is the opposite situation, in which a person can say "no" but cannot say "yes."

How did this come to be?

When the company was small and young, the authority to say "yes" and "no" was vested in one person: The Founder. If you wanted to know if you could do something different, you asked the "One and Only," and you got an answer.

As the company grew bigger and bigger, the founder, or maybe his or her successor, could no longer make every single decision, so some were delegated: He delegated the right to say "no" and kept the right to say "yes" to himself. What did that do? The authority to approve changes migrated up and up in the organizational hierarchy, while the organization was developing layers and layers of "no-sayers." The result: bureaucracy. The organization made changes more and more slowly.

The "livelier" the environment and the faster it changed, the faster the organization was dying.

Authority should be the right to say "yes" *and* "no." If you cannot say "yes," you have no right to say "no." You have to pass the problem and its solution up to where there is authority to say both "yes" *and* "no."

How do you steer a powerboat?

BUT IT IS not only authority that affects whether any changes in a company can be managed. You also have to manage the power structure, which often does not match the authority structure, and the influence structure, which might have a hierarchy of its own.

In other words, you have to pay attention to all sources of energy that move an organization.

Let me give you an analogy. An organization is like a powerboat. It's not enough to sit on the deck, look at the map, do some strategic planning, and decide that we need to change direction. If we don't also change the relative power of the engines, the boat will continue to go in the same direction.

I once saw a cartoon that illustrated this point well. It was a Viking boat. On one side were very muscular, big rowers. On the other side were skinny, starving rowers. And the captain is musing, "I wonder why we are going in circles."

If you want to change direction, you need to change the responsibility and, thereafter, the authority, power, and influence structures of the company.

Here is an example from my consulting experience: The company was very big in the military electronics business. But the Cold War was ending, military budgets were going down, and the market was drying up, so they needed to get into consumer electronics. They had all the knowledge, but somehow they could not make the change.

They had hired a new MBA graduate and made him the project manager for consumer electronics. That poor guy studied the market and prepared papers, prepared more reports, submitted the reports… Nothing happened.

Why?

Let's look at the organization's structure of responsibilities: Sales and engineering both reported to military electronics, and so did finance, human resources, and even production. (This was not strange because it had been a military electronics company.) They had hired only one person to be the entire "consumer electronics" department. He reported to the president, but no one reported to him, not even a secretary. Everyone else worked for military electronics.

What chance did the consumer electronics project

manager have? None. He was like a pimple on an elephant's rear end: just an annoyance. In meetings, everyone sang the praises of consumer electronics and agreed that they needed to get started, but outside the meetings each manager was protecting his turf. Nothing significant happened. The consumer electronics project manager kept writing reports, explaining his beautiful charts and tables, and he was absolutely right. Everybody else watched his show, but nothing changed.

You must change the company's structure (responsibility and authority, power, and influence) when your mission or strategy changes. If you don't do that, the organization will continue to pursue the same path it has in the past.

> *Take-home Value No. 11:*
> *Whenever there is change, to maintain integration it is necessary to re-synchronize the mission and strategy, the structure of responsibilities, the structure of authorance, and the reinforcement system. Since change is continual, each time you finish this process you must start over.*

I helped that company by restructuring it into *two* marketing departments: military electronics and consumer electronics. In the middle were engineering and all the other departments; these departments no longer reported to the market manager of military electronics. Both military electronics and consumer electronics had budgets to spend, and with that resource they had to "buy" the services of engineering, etc. Since both had money to spend, whom was the engineering department going to serve? Both. It had to, because now it had two clients, not one.

Do you see how the authorance structure changed? Of course, the military electronics manager did not like me much; he campaigned to have me fired. No surprise there. But if you want to change the direction, you have to change the structure of responsibilities and authority, power, and influence. People are political animals and usually look out for their own interests. Unless you change that, you are not going to change their behavior.

Here is an example from a government agency. In Los Angeles, I consulted to the largest children's protection organization in the world: 3,500 social workers serving children who were abused sexually, emotionally, and/or physically. At the top of the hierarchy was a chief administrator. Reporting to him was the operations department—all the offices, including all the social workers who were treating children. Also reporting to the chief administrator were the planning and accounting departments, government relations, the administrative staff...

Who got the money to start with? *The administrative staff, who raised the funds from government allocations and from grants.* And whom did they take care of first?

Themselves. What funds went to the social workers in the operations department? Only what remained.

With my help, they changed the structure of authority. All the money went first to operations, and operations then "bought" the services of the administrative staff at headquarters. Once operations was able to buy only the services they needed, the bureaucracy shrunk in half.

Here is another example of how vision, values, and mission were not aligned with the structure of responsibilities and authorance. I worked with a real-estate development company. It took them more than twenty years to develop their image as a company that values quality. They were selling homes and apartments to the upper socioeconomic echelon of their city.

The company grew fast, and quality started to suffer. As you might suspect, they accused the quality-control department of being incompetent, although the managers admitted that they had some of the finest quality-control people in the country.

The importance of structure

AS YOU SHOULD be predicting by now, I looked first at the structure. If you can barely walk, asking you about your state of mind is not the first thing to do. The first step is to look at your leg, perhaps take an x-ray to see whether something in the leg's structure has broken or disintegrated.

In general, people do not ascribe enough importance to structure. If the structure is lousy, you can invest millions in training people but it will not work. It's like training three-legged horses to race.

What I found in this company was that in order to save money, i.e., to be more efficient, they also gave the quality-control people the responsibility to monitor the costs and time of construction projects, and had the construction people report to quality control, too.

Now the quality-control people had a conflict of interest. If they focused on saving costs and completing projects faster, they might have to sacrifice quality. If they focused and insisted on quality, it might cost more and there might be delays.

Quality is difficult to measure. Cost and time schedule deviations are easier to track. So guess what these supervisors did? Focused on costs and time, and quality suffered. And since construction reported to them, any quality problems went "unnoticed" until the clients started complaining.

How long does it take to develop a reputation? Years. How long does it take to destroy a reputation? Minutes.

It is not strange that the International Organization for Standardization (ISO) requires that quality control departments report to the CEO. And that is what I did. I also recommended that the quality supervisors be freed from supervising cost and time. Yes, more people had to be hired, but how much would it cost the company to lose their reputation for quality? How much would it cost to reestablish it? And even if they did rebuild their reputation, it would never be the same. It would taste like reheated soup.

As I have been saying so far, re-structuring an organization's division of responsibilities is necessary but not sufficient. Any time there is change, you have to adapt not just your strategy, your mission, and your direction, which will lead you to change responsibilities in the company; you also have to change the structure of authority. That is what the military electronics company did. First, it changed the structure of responsibilities, and then the structure of authority. Both marketing managers had a budget—in other words, the authority—to buy the services of the engineering unit. Engineering was then forced to respond to both managers in order to get the money.

The same was done with the social workers: Money was given first to the operations department, and they bought staff services—instead of giving the staff the money and letting the staff decide how much money to give operations. We reversed the structure of authority.

The hierarchy of information flow

STILL, THAT'S NOT enough. As part of aligning the structure of responsibilities and authority, you have to change the information system: who gets what information and when. Unless you have information, you cannot carry out your responsibilities and your authority is empty.

How you organize the flow of information is one way to clarify where the authority lies. Furthermore, information is one source of power; when people withhold information they are actually exercising power, albeit illegitimately. So the information system has to be as transparent as possible to minimize abuses of power.

Reinforcements, intrinsic and extrinsic

THE FOURTH SUB-SYSTEM, which you have to align with the first three, is the reinforcement system. Once it is clear what the mission and strategy are, and the company has divided responsibilities and structured authorance correctly, the organization should redesign its system to reinforce the desired behavior.

How is that accomplished? Well, what is the most sensitive part of the human body? Do you know? It's not what you think. It is the pocket. You touch a person's pocket, and they understand what you are talking about. You touch the pocket and they say, "Ah, *that's* what you mean!" They understand very quickly what you want to be done.

But not for long: I have discovered in my forty years of consulting that money motivates people for only about two weeks. If you give someone a salary increase, he will feel good for about two weeks, but after that he will start thinking: "What has the company done for me lately?" People get used to a salary increase very quickly. There is a

Serbian expression, "*Svako cudo za tri dana*," which could be translated as "Every miracle is good for three days." After three days, "What now? What are you going to give me next?"

Furthermore, economists have discovered that what feels rewarding is not the actual increase in income but the *rate* of increase. So if you get a 5 percent annual increase in your take-home pay, locking in that rate of increase for, say, five years as part of your contract, then even though it is an increase, it will be taken for granted and thus not considered a reward. You will feel underpaid for five years. What you want is an increased *rate* of increase: If this year you got 5 percent, then next year it had better be more than 5 percent or it will not be rewarding. Even then, it will still be perceived as rewarding for only about two weeks.

In a famous article in the *Harvard Business Review* in 1968, Frederick Herzberg made an even stronger point about the limits of money as a motivator. He said that money is not a motivating factor; when you get it, you take it for granted. But if you do not get what you believe you deserve, it *de*-motivates you.

For someone who is getting too little, it's de-motivating, but for someone who is adequately paid, it's not motivating; it's expected.

For this reason, I don't like the word "rewards," and I think "compensation" is even worse. What are we trying to do with "rewards"? We are trying to cause, or to *reinforce*, a certain behavior. If the "reward" doesn't effectively reinforce the behavior, then we are giving money away for nothing.

Extrinsic reinforcements

SO, LET US now discuss the components of the system of reinforcement. There are two types of reinforcements: extrinsic and intrinsic.

Extrinsic reinforcements have the following characteristics: Getting the job done does not provide any particular rewards on its own; and the value of the reward depends on external verification.

There are two types of extrinsic rewards: pecuniary (monetary) and non-pecuniary.

Pecuniary: The job itself provides no personal satisfaction; your sense of what the job is worth is tied directly to how much money you are paid and how much that money can buy. You could just as easily not do the job at all and still feel fulfilled—as long as you receive a salary that has objective value. Let's say you have a salary of $100,000 a year, but your country is experiencing tremendous inflation, as in prewar Germany, or recently in Serbia. If $100,000 can barely buy you a cup of coffee, it is worthless as a reinforcement of the desired behavior.

Non-pecuniary: This kind of reinforcement has some of the same characteristics as monetary reinforcement—the reinforcement does not derive from performing the task; its perceived value depends on external validation—but in this case, that validation is status instead of money. For instance, a title: "I'm vice-president." You might have a meaningless, boring, repetitive, insignificant job to do, which for some reason comes with a lofty title. The job you do is not rewarding; your behavior is reinforced by how impressed people are by your title.

There are lots of other symbols of status: where you can park your car; how far your office is from the president's office; whether you have your own secretary. These symbols have little or no importance apart from their visibility; what matters is that everybody knows you have them. If I appoint you a vice-president but nobody knows about it, it's not worth anything. It's worth something only if everybody knows you're a vice-president. Extrinsic reinforcements require external verification of their value.

Intrinsic reinforcements

INTRINSIC REINFORCEMENTS ARE just the opposite. Performing the job—the task itself—provides the reinforcement, and external validation is not necessary. This means you *do* need to do the task to be rewarded; if you don't do the task, there is no reward.

There are four types of intrinsic reinforcements: intrinsic task reward, intrinsic potency reward, intrinsic reinforcement from affiliation, and sense of mission.

Intrinsic task reward: Just having the opportunity to do your job is a reward in itself. For instance, I love to lecture and consult. I can fly all night long and then immediately go to work without feeling tired. I just love it. If I'm asked to do accounting, to balance numbers, you might as well shoot me. So this kind of intrinsic reinforcement depends heavily on personal preferences. When you do what you like to do, you're inspired; you gain energy instead of expending it. When you do something you hate, on the other hand, you feel sapped of energy. So the task itself is a motivator: I love what I do, and to reward me, just let me do it.

Intrinsic potency reward: When you exercise your power over other people, you feel rewarded. In other words, even if you do not like the task, the fact that you can do it and control the people involved is a source of reinforcement. It makes you feel potent.

Intrinsic reinforcement from affiliation: Each time that people affiliate, establish friendship and close relationships, they feel a sense of reward. It reinforces their behavior.

Sense of mission: The fourth intrinsic reinforcement, which I failed to recognize for many years, is the most important. Many years ago, during the Vietnam War, I was consulting for the prime minister of Peru. I was lecturing on the subject of rewards, and somebody in the audience asked, "Doctor Adizes, are the Vietnamese fighting the Americans because they get paid very well [i.e., for extrinsic pecuniary rewards]? Are they mercenaries?"

I said, "No."

"Are they fighting you because they like to parade

on the first of May, wounded, without legs but with lots of decorations, and hear everybody applauding [i.e., for extrinsic non-pecuniary rewards]?"

"I don't think so," I said.

"Are they fighting because they love to fight [intrinsic task reward]? They enjoy fighting and dying?"

Again, I said, "I don't think so."

"Are they fighting because they like to beat the Americans, just to prove the Americans are weak [intrinsic potency reward]?"

"I don't think so."

"Are they fighting because they like fighting together and the joy of camaraderie they get in close combat [intrinsic reinforcement from affiliation]?"

"No, that is not it."

"So why are they fighting?"

"Oh!" I said. "Because of their mission! They have a purpose in life: to unify Vietnam."

This is the fourth intrinsic reinforcement: the fulfillment of a mission in which one wholeheartedly believes.

Now let us look at some examples to understand these rewards better.

What do you call people who get no, or very minimal, salary; no salary increases for long periods of time; no recognition; terrible tasks under terrible conditions—in the jungle, plagued by mosquitoes, malaria, all kinds of other diseases, where the locals actually try to kill them? What are these people called? *Missionaries.* They do it because of their mission. People in general will go to war and even die for their mission. Nothing else, just the mission. Thus, fulfilling a mission, having and advancing a mission, is the most powerful and gratifying reward there is. People will take little or no money, work under terrible conditions, overcome feeling powerless for a period of time, overcome rejection, overcome aggression, anything, and keep going. Why? Because they have a mission.

Which people receive little or no salary, live in tenements, and can't afford to eat well? They have no power or recognition (though they dream of future recognition). If you ask them what their mission is, they haven't got the slightest idea. But they love what they do. Who are they? Artists: painters, dancers, musicians. They are compelled to do what they do, even without money or recognition.

Next, and particularly interesting: Who does not receive salary increases for long periods, gets no recognition, whose task is unpleasant, repetitive, and menial? They have no mission or do not feel strongly about it, or even know what it is. But they are very potent. Power is their only reward. Who are they? Bureaucrats. Their only reward is to wield power over the people who come to them for help: "Come back tomorrow." "You don't have the right form." "You are standing in the wrong line." "Bring this again next week." "Go stand over there." "Wait." "Your documentation is incomplete." They can make you go back and forth all day long. The fact that they can make you do whatever they order you to do is their reward. This type of person might also be a warden in a prison: Salary is not the motivator; nor is there any recognition. Their only reward is being allowed to control the prisoners, to feel superior to them.

Next type: Their mission is vague, their power limited, to say the least. The task may be interesting but it's not the reason to do it. The pay is limited or not growing. The only benefit is the non-pecuniary reward, status. Who is that? The cheap politician.

How about people who really do not have a mission, no salary, no status outside their own group, who have a sense of power although it is illegitimate, and whose task itself is not gratifying. Their sense of reward—what reinforces their behavior—is affiliation, the belonging to each other. Who are they? Gangs.

And one more: They don't know their mission, have no power and have to avoid even the appearance of wielding power. They repeat one task over and over, all day long, every day. There is no recognition, none: You're nobody. You get a salary and that's it. Who are they? Workers! Yes, workers, the majority of people on this planet.

Should we be surprised that workers strike, that they sabotage the factory machines? When they do that, they feel at least somewhat powerful and as if they have a mission, if only for the duration of the strike.

The value of empowerment

THINK ABOUT THIS: In general, mission is more rewarding than salary. Salary rewards for only two weeks; mission for much longer. Do the people in your company have a mission that is more than just words put together to sound good? A real mission, to do something real for someone else? Furthermore, can you make your people feel empowered? Can you have participative management? Do people have a chance to talk? Is there a forum for complaints and communication? Someone they can talk to about their problems, someone who can help solve them?

> *Take-home Value No. 12:*
>
> *Intrinsic rewards are the best system of reinforcements. The more intrinsic rewards, the less relative need for extrinsic rewards.*

Empower your people. They are more than hands; they are brains, too. Give them a sense of mission and recognition, an opportunity to be heard, and they will give their lives to you. When people know where they are going and can contribute to the decision-making, if they love what they are doing, then money is much less important. On the other hand, if they have no idea where and why the company is going wherever it is going; if they have no power and receive no recognition; if the task is boring and repetitive; and the only thing they get is a salary with fringe benefits (which are usually considered part of a salary), you will have to pay them a lot, and whatever you pay still will not be enough. They will always complain and ask for more.

Warren Shmid, a colleague of mine from many years ago at UCLA, had an interesting parable.

As we all know, golfers are aficionados. They are truly dedicated to the game. How could you frustrate them so badly that eventually they would come to hate the game?

First, you do not let them decide which golf club to use. They do not have a say about it: "The engineering department studied what you need, and you should use this one now."

Then, they cannot see the hole. A manager only points out a direction. The player hits the ball in that direction, but as soon as the ball takes off, a curtain falls down and he has no idea what happened to the ball. If the ball lands in the right place, the player hears nothing about it. If it lands far away from the hole, he gets reprimanded, maybe even ejected from the course and not allowed to play there anymore.

Would you like to play golf like that? You do not know what the goals are. You do not know what results you get. You have not have a say in how to do it, either. It would not be strange if this golfer hit the ball directly at the head of the manager standing near the curtain. At least then he'd get some feedback.

But isn't that how we manage?

What could go wrong?

IN ORDER TO be strong, these four sub-systems must be dealt with—preferably proactively, to avoid disintegration. They get out of balance very fast. An organization is like a very sensitive car: its parts get out of alignment quickly, and that's when things start to go wrong.

What, exactly, could go wrong? Take the reinforcement sub-system. Let's say your neighbor got a salary increase, while you haven't had one in a long time. Or the rate of inflation is rising rapidly, and you feel your rewards haven't kept up with inflation. By the way, I want you to know something: *Nobody* feels he or she is being sufficiently rewarded financially—even if he makes millions a year, or a day. And we know the reasons: Increased pay has an impact for two weeks; what is perceived to be rewarding is the rate of increase, rather than the absolute number, and by definition the rate of increase cannot be infinite.

What else could go wrong? The environment has changed, rendering your mission and strategy increasingly irrelevant. Or the structure of responsibilities, established sometime in the past, no longer adequately addresses the requirements of the mission and strategy of the future. Or authority might be too centralized to react quickly to local situations.

All these discontinuities occur because the external situation has changed. What we have from the past does not align with what we have in the present and what we will have in the future.

Finally, the reinforcement system could be reinforcing the wrong behaviors and penalizing the right ones: For instance, the organization is still rewarding individual achievement, while under the new structure the need is for teamwork. In that case, the reinforcement sub-system is reflecting the needs of the past rather than the present and future.

All of these sub-systems vibrate with change and reconfigure themselves constantly. The authority and responsibility structures are not steady; they're always moving. Perhaps a co-worker is replaced by somebody who clearly is more powerful than your previous collaborator; that alone might be enough to make you feel less powerful, because now you have to contend with him.

And don't forget that responsibilities change as the market changes. They—along with your strategy and your tactics—cannot remain fixed. That's why the people in any organization cannot be happy all the time or even for very long. If these four sub-systems were fixed and equal—if everything were perfect for too long—that would mean there had been no change. And you know what that means: You are dead.

In organizations that are alive, people are periodically unhappy. If they are alive they are changing, and change is always accompanied by stress. There is a questionnaire psychologists use in which they award a certain number of stress points for different events: losing a job, so many points; divorce, so many points; death in the immediate family, so many points; going on vacation, so many points.

What is the common denominator? Change. So the more agile a company is, the more it changes, and the more stressed the people are—unless the four sub-systems are realigned, unless people believe the organization will be realigned, unless there is hope that the misery of not being able to correctly fulfill their responsibilities, or not being adequately reinforced, will be dealt with.

> *Take-home Value No. 13:*
>
> *If everybody in your organization is content for too long, the organization might not be dynamic enough; it may be failing to deal with change. The only other explanation is that you are already doing the right thing: constantly aligning and realigning the sub-systems.*

In companies that are dead, people *are* happy. In bureaucracies, I always find lots of complacent people. Because nothing new is happening. I believe there were probably more happy people in Russia under Communism than in the capitalistic system today, because under Communism nothing new ever happened; everything was frozen. Beyond the face they showed the world—Sputnik, the atomic bomb—their technology was frozen. Their industrial parks were completely outdated. Their art was frozen. They were poor. But they appeared content unless they had a need to speak up.

What do you, as a leader, need to do? You have to be a good mechanic, constantly fixing your organization. It's a demanding job. Restructure the organizational chart, redefine authority, redo the rewards, redo the strategy, start again. If you don't, the sub-systems will get permanently out of balance and out of control, and that's when people lose hope and say, "Nothing works around here." If you have any experience managing anything, you know what happens when people lose hope and get apathetic.

We should have seen it coming

A GOOD EXAMPLE OF the sub-systems' disintegration is the current financial crisis, which a lot of people predicted. But even though people saw it coming, nobody knew whose responsibility it was to try to fix it. Nobody knew who had the authority to make the numerous changes necessary to avoid a crisis. Lots of people were reaping rewards from riding the wave of short-term profit, while it was unclear who, if anyone, would be rewarded for intervening to prevent the crisis.

How do I know that the problems were predictable? In 1982, I was consulting for Bank of America. At that time it was one of the largest banks in the world, with $120 billion in assets, but it was very bureaucratic. It was losing market share and going downhill. They needed to change direction, and they invited me to help.

I spent three years consulting there. I worked closely

with one of the top executives, and one evening over a drink, he disclosed something that really surprised me. He said: "Ichak, we don't know what's going on anymore. With all these cash derivatives, and cash equivalents, and all the new financial instruments, we are losing control. We know less and less what is going on."

I once flew with Mike Milken, the "king" of junk bonds who went to prison for securities fraud in the 1980s. I asked him: "Mike, when did you know you were going to go to prison?"

"A long time before they even charged me," he said.

"How come?"

"Because I was issuing so many junk bonds, I knew the government was getting worried. They didn't know how to handle this new phenomenon. It *was* a new phenomenon, and if you don't have any precedent, you don't know what's going to happen. They were afraid that if junk bonds massively defaulted they might have a domino effect on the economy. So they had to stop me somehow and were looking for an excuse. And they found it. And I saw it coming."

We escaped the potential disaster of junk bonds, but the vast changes in capital market structures were still evolving. The roots of the current financial crisis, as in the 1980s, involve a number of unprecedented phenomena in the history of financial services. I would even say that economic reality outpaced economic theory. There was little or nothing in economic theory that dealt with this subject. Nobody was looking at the totality, because at least some of it had never happened before.

So the crash had to happen. But as I said earlier, those who know what to do in a crisis will come out winners. And those who don't know what to do will be lost in the desert.

"Fish-scale society"

THE WORLD WE live in is not only changing faster and faster, it's also growing more intense. From the "atomistic" (separate) societies we once had, we are moving into a "fish-scale" society. What does this mean? If you look at the scales of a fish, you will see they overlap. Everything is starting to overlap. And it's happening everywhere. That's why there is so much intensity: Economic problems are also political problems, political problems are also social problems. Technological changes and problems have an impact on societies, economics, and politics. Nothing is separate anymore. Everything is interrelated.

At universities in the not so distant past, there were separate departments of biology, chemistry, mathematics, sociology, anthropology. Today you have chemical biology and physical mathematics and socio-anthropology. What is going on? Everything is overlapping.

You can see it even in current fashion: It is called "unisex." Men and women have the same haircut. They wear the same clothes.

And in politics, more and more, national boundaries exist only on maps. They don't exist in reality. Why? Because air doesn't recognize borders: I live in California, but I breathe the pollution that is created in China. The wind brings the pollution from China all the way to California.

Water doesn't know boundaries, either. Pollute the water there and it will affect us here. You cannot stop television stations from broadcasting across borders. Radio, too, goes across borders. So what does "border" mean anymore? What significance can it have in the new reality we live in? Where are the security guards who hermetically protect the border?

> *Take-home Value No. 14:*
> *Because our world is growing ever more interdependent, we need integrating, systemic solutions.*

The problem is that, although in reality we are living in a global society, we still think as isolated entities. We don't know how to work together. Even the United Nations is just an accumulation of numerous national interests. Nobody really represents the globe as a unified entity. Nobody worries about interdependency; everybody is watching out for himself. While everything on the planet is becoming interrelated, we still think atomistically and our global institutions reflect it. This will become more and more of a problem, manifesting itself as a global crisis. Because we live in a fish-scale environment, financial crises will have political and social repercussions that will be crises all by themselves.

Another way to put it is that our problems are becoming more and more systemic. Systemic problems call for systemic solutions, for which we need systemic leaders and systemic guidance to assist those leaders. That's why you cannot solve a crisis just by firing 20 percent of your people; that's like liposuction. You need to work with all the sub-systems in your company. If you're a prime minister, you have to work on all the components of the society—economic, technological, social—all at the same time. And that's a tall order.

That's why I see the need for a paradigm shift in our management education. We don't have enough systemic education. We teach too much *functional* education—too much finance, economics, accounting, marketing, human resources. But who is looking at the totality? *That* is true management education. And that's what we need.

Changing values, changing behavior

AT THE BEGINNING of this book, crisis was defined as a major departure point where you have to make a choice. The word originates from Greek and means: You are now in a situation where you have to make a serious choice. Not more or less of the same, but different.

A crisis does not call for linear thinking. It means reinventing the system, not just tinkering with the system. In managerial parlance, this is not a case of continuous improvement. It is time for new product development and may even be time for new technology development.

I think the materialism and greed for more, more, more, money, money, money, is working against us. You often need this "make money, make money" motivation to build something. We needed greed and economic materialism to build the country. It is OK for the beginning stages of the lifecycle. But if we continue like this, as America is doing, the system that has built the country will destroy the country. The "business model" is working against us now: We are polluting the air, we are polluting the earth, we are polluting the water, we are creating destructive waste. And, sadly, we are not even having fun: When I work in a developing country, I hear more laughter in one day than I hear in a whole year in a developed country. People have no time to laugh. Everybody is working, time is money, we have to make more, more, more, and more.

But more, more, more, is not better; sometimes you raise the standard of living, but lower the quality of life. So we need to change our goals and our direction. Our goal has always been economic growth, and that is what we measured. Economic growth became a religion.

Somebody recently asked me, "If we change our values, will economic growth stop?" I said, "I hope so." Because more is not better; more is becoming less. You can already see it in the developed and developing countries: two cars in the family, three cars in the family—and what's happening on the streets? Traffic. Pollution. The standard of living is going up; the quality of life, down.

We have to change our goals as a society, from better standard of living to better quality of life. To measure quality of life, we can use social indicators: divorce rate, crime, teen pregnancies, how many kids finish high school. We have to take our eyes away from economic growth and focus instead on social goals.

> *Take-home Value No. 15:*
>
> *It's time for the developed countries to recognize that at a certain point, the quality of life diminishes as the standard of living increases.*

Economic growth is right and cash is important, but only up to a point. If you have already built the country, it's time to say, "Enough is enough." There are some very smart people who have already said, "Enough! I have a house, I have a car, I have enough. Now I want to live." It's the same for a country. Now we have to live better.

Summing up

CHANGE IS INEVITABLE, as long as we are alive. This has always been true; what's different is that today, changes happen more frequently, and more intensely, and thus we face more problems with increasing frequency. Because we are increasingly interdependent, a problem over there will almost immediately be felt here.

Whenever there is change, there are problems, which are caused by disintegration. Disintegration is what happens when an organization's sub-systems get out of alignment. This theory applies not only to companies but to individuals, families, and nations. One of the worst aspects of our current disintegration is that our social values have been slow to respond to technological progress, and that has left us without a moral framework for dealing with the ethical issues that technology raises.

Problems that are not treated become crises. But whether they're dealing with problems or crises, strong organizations will take the steps to become stronger, while weak companies will freeze, wait, or not know what to do. Or they will take only partial measures, which is like taking some but not all of the medicine you need to take. This kind of behavior can be fatal.

Crisis is a disaster for the weak, but an opportunity for the strong, because if there were no change, the mediocre would catch up. Thus, strong companies welcome a crisis, which tends to weed out the competition.

And what does it mean to be stronger? It means being

able to deal successfully with change, faster and better than your competition. For that, you need integration; integration is the cure for disintegration, which is the by-product of change. Continually align and realign the four sub-systems. It is not enough to do it once and then go back to business as usual. It is a never-ending task.

Integration should happen on multiple levels: within yourself, with your family and friends, and with your employees and clients.

It is better to deal with a crisis proactively, preparing for the problems that are typical for that stage. If it is too late to do this proactively, it can also be done reactively. Essentially, you must adapt to the changing environment by aligning the four sub-systems of the organization: mission and strategy, responsibilities, authority, and reinforcement, in that order. At the same time, you have to monitor your bloodstream: your cash.

One way a strong company deals with a crisis is by circling the wagons and fighting the enemy together. To do that, people in the organization must trust one another. But trust cannot be developed in an instant; it must be nurtured over time, or else it will not be there when it is needed.

In a crisis, it is crucial to maintain cash flow and protect your human capital. The usual tendency is to fire people in order to cut costs. That's not the best thing to do, because people comprise the muscles and brains of your organization, and are the main component of your organization's culture. Culture is very difficult to build and maintain; therefore, firing people should be your last resort. If you find you must cut labor costs, cut people's hours instead of cutting people; that way, you will hold onto your assets while diffusing the financial pain among all of the employees.

If you keep your people and they have extra time, assign them to improve and reengineer the company's products and strategies. After all, your company suddenly has time to think, which it did not have when it was overwhelmed with work in a growing economy.

Make the crisis a turning point for your company to strengthen relationships and to innovate.

Because our environment is becoming increasingly interrelated (a fish-scale society), our problems are becoming increasingly systemic and require systemic solutions, for which we need systemic leaders and systemic consultants. This is why our management educational system needs to change its main focus from function (finance, economics, marketing, etc.) to looking at the totality, the system.

About the Adizes Institute

FOR THE PAST 35 years, the Adizes Institute has been committed to equipping visionary leaders, management teams, and agents of change to become champions of their industry and markets. These leaders have successfully established a collaborative organizational culture by using Adizes' pragmatic tools and concepts to achieve peak performance.

Adizes specializes in guiding leaders of organizations (CEOs, top management teams, boards, owners) to quickly and effectively resolve issues such as:

- Difficulties in executing good decisions.
- Making the transition from entrepreneurship to professional management.
- Difficulties in aligning the structure of the organization to achieve its strategic intent.
- Bureaucratizing: when an organization is getting out of touch with its markets and losing entrepreneurial vitality.
- Conflicts among founders, owners, board members, partners, and family members.
- Internal management team conflicts and "politics" severe enough to inhibit the success of the business.
- Growing pains.
- "Culture clashes" between companies undergoing mergers or acquisitions.

Adizes also offers comprehensive training and certification for change leaders who wish to incorporate into their practice the Adizes methodologies for managing change.

Adizes is the primary sponsor of the Adizes Graduate School, a nonprofit teaching organization that offers Master's and Ph.D. programs for the Study of Leadership and Change.

For more information about these and other programs, please visit www.adizes.com.

Selected complementary works by Dr. Adizes

Recommended videos: Bottom-Line Management Excerpts Video Series, Santa Barbara, CA: Adizes Institute Publications, 2006.

1. How to Define an Organization's Mission (18:33 min)
2. What is First: Strategy or Structure? (23:24 min)
3. The Signs of Organizational Aging (13:09 min)
4. From Entrepreneurship to Professional Management (24:32 min)
5. Management and Mismanagement Styles (32:40 min)
6. How to Hire the Right People (21:25 min)
7. How to Delegate (13:38 min)
8. The Ideal Executive (19:06 min)
9. What is a Leader? (16:33 min)
10. The Secret of Success of Any Organization (25:36 min)

Recommended books

Managing Corporate Lifecycles: An Updated and Expanded Look at the Classic Work CORPORATE LIFECYCLES. Adizes Institute Publications, 2004

The Ideal Executive: Why You Cannot Be One and What To Do About It: A New Paradigm for Management. Leadership Trilogy Vol 1. Adizes Institute Publications, 2004.

Management/Mismanagement Styles: How to Identify a Style and What to Do about It. Leadership Trilogy Vol 2. Adizes Institute Publications, 2004.

Leading the Leaders: How to Enrich Your Style of Management and Handle People Whose Style is Different from Yours. Leadership Trilogy Vol 3. Adizes Institute Publications, 2004.

The Pursuit of Prime. Knowledge Exchange, 1996.

Mastering Change: The Power of Mutual Trust and Respect in Personal Life, Family, Business and Society. Adizes Institute Publications, 1993.

How to Solve the Mismanagement Crisis. Adizes Institute Publications, 1980